W9-ARH-192

INTERVALS

BOOKS

Poetry

And Autumn Came
Stanyan Street & Other Sorrows
Listen to the Warm
Lonesome Cities
In Someone's Shadow
Caught in the Quiet
Fields of Wonder
And to Each Season
Come to Me in Silence
Moment to Moment
Celebrations of the Heart
Beyond the Boardwalk
The Sea Around Me
Coming Close to the Earth
We Touch the Sky
The Power Bright & Shining
The Beautiful Strangers
The Sound of Solitude
Suspension Bridge
Valentines
Intervals

Collected Poems

Twelve Years of Christmas
A Man Alone
With Love
The Carols of Christmas

Seasons in the Sun
Alone
The Rod McKuen Omnibus
Hand in Hand
Love's Been Good to Me
Looking for a Friend
Too Many Midnights
Watch for the Wind

Prose

Finding My Father

Et Cetera

A Book of Days
A Book of Days, 2
Another Beautiful Day
Another Beautiful Day, 2

Music Collections

New Carols for Christmas
The McKuen/Sinatra Songbook
New Ballads
At Carnegie Hall
28 Greatest Hits
Through European Windows
The Songs of Rod McKuen, 1
The Songs of Rod McKuen, 2

BY ROD McKUEN

MUSIC

Concertos

For Piano & Orchestra
For Cello & Orchestra
For Guitar & Orchestra
#2 for Piano & Orchestra
For Four Harpsichords
Seascapes for Piano
The Woodwinds

Symphonies, Symphonic Suites, etc.

Symphony No. 1
Ballad of Distances
The City
Piano & String Suites
Adagio for Harp & Strings
Rigadoon for Orchestra
Pastures Green/Pavements
   Gray
Symphony No. 4

Chamber

Piano Trios
Piano Quartets
Sonata for Ondes Martenot

Ballet

Americana, R.F.D.

Point/Counterpoint
Elizabethan Dances
The Minotaur (Man to
   Himself)
Volga Song
Full Circle
The Plains of My Country
The Man Who Tracked the
   Stars
Birch Trees
Liberty
I'm Not Afraid (with Jacques
   Brel)
Seven Cynical Songs
Dance Your Ass Off

Major Film Scores

The Prime of Miss Jean Brodie
A Boy Named Charlie Brown
Joanna
The Unknown War
Scandalous John
The Borrowers
Lisa Bright & Dark
Emily
Travels with Charley
The Beach
Imaginary Landscapes

with drawings by the author

HARPER & ROW, PUBLISHERS, New York
Cambridge, Philadelphia, San Francisco, Washington
London, Mexico City, São Paulo, Singapore, Sydney

CHEVAL BOOKS, Los Angeles
Sydney, Amsterdam

ROD McKUEN

INTERVALS

Some of this material appeared in different form in *Folio, Opus 10,* and the *Times Supplement.* "Is There Life After Tower Records?" is from a work in progress. A variation of "Have You Been to Holland?" first appeared in *Another Beautiful Day.*

"Lament" is from *The New Grove Dictionary of Music and Musicians,* © 1980, Macmillan Publishers Limited. Used by permission. All rights reserved.

INTERVALS. Copyright © 1986 by Rod McKuen and Montcalm Productions, Inc. Artwork © 1986 by Rod McKuen. All rights reserved. Printed in the United States of America. No part of this book may be used or reproduced in any manner whatsoever without written permission except in the case of brief quotations embodied in critical articles and reviews. For information address Harper & Row, Publishers, Inc., 10 East 53rd Street, New York, N.Y. 10022 or Cheval Books, P.O. Box 2783, Hollywood, CA 90028. Published simultaneously in Canada by Fitzhenry & Whiteside Limited, Toronto.

FIRST EDITION

Designed by Ruth Bornschlegel

Library of Congress Cataloging-in-Publication Data

McKuen, Rod.
  Intervals.

  Includes index.
  I. Title.
PS3525.A264154   1986   811'.54   86-45126
ISBN 0-06-015635-X

86 87 88 89 90 HC 10 9 8 7 6 5 4 3 2 1

For Lydia Brandt

1: INTERVALS

Intervals *3*

Interval Between *11*

On the Highway *16*

Suicide Is Risky *19*

Here the Eagle *20*

Short Story *24*

Still Life with Baroque Worries *28*

2: SHADOW PLAYERS

Movers *33*

Mr. Peel's Way *37*

Rimbaud's Sister *44*

To the Memory of Stan Kamen *49*

Passing Over *54*

Los Hombres *56*

Lion Watch *58*

Pierrot Lunaire *59*

CONTENTS

Variety Artist *62*

Still Life with Rubber Washer *64*

3: IS THERE LIFE AFTER TOWER RECORDS?

Is There Life After Tower Records? *71*

Still Life with Horne and Sills *103*

4: THE LOWER FORTY

Pacing Off the Lower Forty *111*

Radio *120*

Outside Tres Vidas (A Memory, January 1975) *122*

Have You Been to Holland? *130*

First You Take a Live Goat *132*

Modern Romance *133*

Still Life After All These Years *137*

INDEX OF FIRST LINES *143*

interval: A pause or break
in the course of something.

1

Intervals

Intervals

I close the windows
fire the furnace
begin to heat the bath.
The crawling things come out.
Great tangles of spiders,
            small and friendly,
arrive from no place
(once started
        long-abandoned
                manuscripts,
books arranged by subject matter
                and thus useless).
They forage over Compact Discs,
scale picture frames
        to skate along the glass.
One climbs a clock,
another drops a silken cord
from wooden eagle's shoulder.
One more pops from half-read Dickens
            a gas bill page mark falls.
Termites carried from the woodpile
            flee from kindling.
Moths flap and bat at table lamps,
                do highland flings
and smack against the windowglass.

Orchid bulbs are popping open,
like time-lapse photographs.
Older blossoms move to sooner death.
A line of piss-ants
come and go along the stalks
get trapped in gooey nectar bait.
Wall spiders wait until each ant
is icy, frosty-covered, eclair-like
before they start
their choc-o-holic gorge
on the snared remains.

The heat now renders
all three cats
languid, lazy, droopy-tailed
and finally dead to morning sleep.
Bingo's on his back again, flat-out
all four paws hang in a halfway stretch
                    toward the ceiling.
Nikki sneezes and rolls over.

I take another crack
at ciphering a Schoenberg score.
        My pencil breaks.

I fail to write another letter,
let one more deadline pass
(five hundred words on Barenboim's
six-disc survey of Mozart sonatas).
I start another lengthy list
                of things undone
that once set down will be forgotten,
filed from one high stack of papers
                        to another,
to then be pushed along
and added to another box of *stuff;*
unopened invitations, calendar pages,
last year's etceteras unreturned.
Here are Christmas cards
addressed last year to special people,
set aside for special notes
that stay unwritten.
Over there two clipped obituaries
with marginal notes about condolence calls.
A too-expensive koala bear
                that Helen gave me
squats high above the clutter on my desk
where I can always see it.
A reminder of hallucinogen days
not gone yet, only different.

GROVE 10, Kern to Lindelheim,
lies open on the table at *Lament:*

Ceremonial laments performed by men are not
unknown, but as a rule the task is entrusted to
women, most often the close relatives of the
dead person; sometimes, however, specialist
keeners are invited to mourn. They may be
regarded, in some degree, as professionals.
Generally they are women of prestige in the
village, with a known talent for keening, who
are invited to funerals to lead or augment the
lamenting. If they are paid at all, it is likely to
be in kind, rarely in money.

A five-year garden diary
that's been around for three
                looks brand-new.
I plant, I weed, I harvest,
but never write about it.
I turn from musing (odd word that)
to an article on psychic cats
                Wade clipped for me.
I discover a paragraph
        started yesterday,
wad it up and overshoot
              the wastebasket.
It lands just this side of a shiny tin
ramshead ice bucket full of day-old
                tepid water.

Maybe I should take up drinking again.
But, no, there is no time to get it right.
When writers turn to alcohol
they must become Great Alcoholics,
                    or what's the point?

A bold, gray eagle head,
          a Larry/Walter gift,
sits high above a bookcase
          and surveys domain.
His eye looks on and over
          old oak four-poster bed,
one small corner used by me.
The rest devoted to *Times, Herald,
Times*—a week's worth—books,
notes to no one, more CDs,
TV zapper, letters, scratch pad,
Magic's ear-mite prescription,
March *Schwann,* April *Gramophone.*

Nearby a chair
almost as old as me. The cats
have clawed it till it needs
                    intensive care.
Coffee mugs are everywhere.
A toy the cats are bored with
has found a corner to its liking,
it lies there with a fading catnip smile.

Mismatched stereo components
vie with used but unmarked videos
                    for the dust's attention.
On one speaker, *Bulfinch Mythology*
becomes a sandwich in between
                    a few more Compact Discs.
Near an unattended telephone
a rolodex lies wounded on its side.

Unused tickets to last weekend's
                    Previn concert
have joined orange peelings
                    for a still life.
They await the brush, the knife,
                    the shutter click
for layered immortality.

Another letter to the painter
                    started on graph pad
is lost but not forgotten.
A mended pair of reading glasses.
A Winston Churchill oncidium
carried from the greenhouse
needs a shave and trim
before it can be termed respectable.

Reading glasses on the nightstand
atop well-worn Thomas Aquinas.
On the mantel, reading glasses
nearly covered by unopened mail,
                              circulars,
                              catalogues,
                cruise ship itineraries,
                         land auctions,
the stuff of somebody else's dreams.

The radio is singing
What's the use of wonderin'?
I switch it off and play Corelli
                on the phonograph.
Satisfied and thankful
                    for the gadgets in my life
I turn it up and push the replay button.
Elizabeth is coming for the weekend.
Helen wants an outline.
        Francis wants a meeting.
Charles thinks we ought to start
                a poet/actor workshop.
Do I know Chuck Heston?
            He knows Mickey Shaughnessy.

Edward slipped a note beneath the door,
let's go shopping.
Someday, maybe.
When the work's all done
            and every bill's been paid,
I'll exchange a deadline for a lifeline.
I'll go shopping then. Vacation then.

Spring arrives officially tomorrow.
            I let the fire go out.

Interval Between

In the interval
between bed sitting chair
              and bed
your silhouette
is growing fainter
shifting as it moves
through distance.
I lapse into a momentary dream,
too soft for sustenance
              too hard
for mere impression.
And still you are
              the landscape
all of it.

These quiet minutes
              with you
before and after
what should have been
or could be making love
are firmer than
what arms encircle
as the vaulted premium
in the act itself.

Earlier a petal fell
from off a dying rose.
It hit the table
with such thunder
I thought the neighborhood
            would be aroused.
You didn't move.
And down the street
no lights came on.
The darkness turns upon
                    itself.
Your breathing
is the only music left,
its rise and fall hypnotic.

There is something delicate,
                    mysterious
in the interval
from breath to breath
as there is in between
bed sitting chair and bed.

The stars
have started coming out,
like Christmas finery,
unhurried and unstoppable.
In the tree outside
the same owl croons
        the same song
this one time more.
His call is loonlike
and still no tune comes back
from crossblock tree.
Not far off another owl
and rows of lesser birds
        sit quietly
in rapt appreciation.
And now a cat has gotten up
to stetch and drink
        and paw cymbidium
overripe and sleeping in its pot.
Your breathing takes
        a new direction.

There is something,
                if not everything,
loose and wandering about
each breath you take
                and then give up
as there is an interval between
half empty bed
and bed sitting chair.

The flame released
is never in proportion
to the fire quenched.
The way a photograph
a moment after being taken
drops the subject caught.

Your shadow moves from you.
Up against the wall it goes
then arching out
                across the ceiling
down it comes
to settle on another wall.

Stars now strafe the room
               with starlight
enough to close the gap
around your shadow
coming back to you/us.
Enough to fill the interval
               that separated
bed sitting chair from bed.

On the Highway

We drive back late from supper
through miles of unlit roads
fields flat if we could see them.
Bound for home; familiar colors, milk,
bed and safety, retinue, routine.
Near midnight we lose our way
take a different road deliberately.
                    What used to be adventure
is now the nothing-left-to-chance
                                    excursion.

The lap of the Gods
is uncomfortable.
Especially on the highway.

A pickup truck
full of laughing adolescents
rolls by and nearly rolls us
                    off the road.
Long after they have passed
their faces linger in the darkness.
So young, so alien to us.
Youth ought to be more careful
if it wants to reach old age.

On through the black
and still we do not speak.
Home to milk. Warm milk now
                    and bed.
You go on thinking I stole your youth
deprived you of your pickup truck,
your pick-up-sticks experience.
We do not need reminders here
of me as bandit, you the victim.
The Accusation
spreads across your eyes in daylight,
floods from them at night.

A flashing roadsign
illuminates your face for seconds.
It is pale, lovely. Lost.
My failure to accommodate
                    and please
has grown on you,
is now an awful beauty mark of age,
a worryline both grooved and pegged—
a part of your features for always.
Nothing in your face cries out defeat
but condemnation's posted everywhere.

The silence lengthens.
It ought to be a richer language.
The wafer passed from hand to tongue
should not need connecting sentence,
only the wine to wash it down,
only the muttering later.

You were my charm against nightmares,
the battering ram to knock down silence.
I was the knight who stumbled,
                on somebody else's ground.

Suicide Is Risky

Autumn comes early
the bracken is red.
The wind takes my hat
to another street.
The hills are all naked,
the trees wetted down
and the rivers
are finding new rivers.

You are the legend.
I am the fable.
Fall finds us sitting
at separate tables.

Here the Eagle

FOR NATHANIEL TARN

Here the eagle lost and weary
turns white head again to survey
acres of some new-flown land.
Seeing no branch broad enough
for his frame to rest upon
he ascends another hundred feet
and lets the jet stream push him on.

Eagles were not born
          to stumble
on the atmosphere,
they use air to stride upon.
To make a mighty pride of eagles,
          it takes only one.
Spreading wings the length of Egypt,
tails that fan out, width of Gael,
claws that cause the rock to shudder
          when the eagle fastens on.

Jeweled tongue of fearsome eagle
sounds alarm to lark and dove.
A mile below the snow mole hurries
to his deeper chamber where
even safety of the burrow
would not tempt an eagle dare.
Crows cease cawing. Blackbird hides
in the cornfield where his strutting
made him minstrel of the minute
till his eye caught eagle's flight.

Onward, onward, finally there
a wood where pine and cedar meet,
letting no sun greet the vine
that rises up from yellow grass
to steal the light from lower limb.
A glide then
            not so much a dive
then landing silent, but for shadow
like a cloud that sails and stops
the eagle drops in unannounced.

Eagles who have dozed in Spain
tell lesser birds it's Babylon
as they sail off to Bogotá,
Colombia, and farther on.

Every eagle has a destiny
(known to only God and him)
that unfulfilled brings laceration
to eternity's round rim.

Eagles flapping leather wings
scatter sparrow, loon migrations,
race the moon at twilight hour,
         shiver under hunter's glare.
When one dies, the sky falls down.
And nothing's left above but air.

And now the morning hikes
                    from seashore
climbs through mists
            too dense for stars
who one by one begin to fail
like candles in the Santa Ana.
It's then the eagle skims the ocean,
dive-bombs the greener islands and
gleans the sand for open clam.
Then after feast preens talon,
tangled underbody hair,
sniffs the air and turns,
eyes and head raised heavenward.

In the rise and fall of things
done by nature to a turn,
eagles have to be the summit
of what creation's so far learned.

Short Story

FOR SAM CROCKER

The old A train
did not just make
the San Francisco/Oakland run,
it traveled half around
         the Oakland Bay.
A set of unpunched transfers
found amid the gutter litter
could be redeemed for romance rides
daytrips lasting half a day.

A wave at someone,
         no one waving back
from like train passing by,
a smile imagined from a neighborhood,
a frown deflected with an eye blink,
contact made without contact—
could push a little dream beyond
imaginary boundaries set and taught
by those without imaginations.

I saw her first
deftly stepping platform steps
                at the Lakeside stop,
rummaging through her pocketbook
for change or something smaller
                than a Lincoln bill.
Hair, not hair at all, but something else,
eyes without a smudge of camouflage.
She came down the aisle toward me
                and then passed.

Six stops and she was getting up to go.
                I barely made it
through the folding door behind her
without my shirttail being caught.
She transferred to the Ashcroft train.
                I transferred too.

By now I knew she must have caught
my little glance, then open stare.
I still remember those white shoulders
barely covered by a cotton dress
and how when she shrugged out of thought
they moved, rose up, rose up again
and caused her breasts to gently brush
                          the summer sundress,
her flesh as gentle to the cotton
                as bee to blossom.
Would I were the dress, I thought,
                     against the skin,
my head the head that next would lie
against the flesh released from dress.

Summer wishes. Many summers gone.
Summer daydreams, life sails out upon.

And I remember that the sun
                          was spinning,
sending tracer bullet beams
through my bus window blinding me
                          to everything
but that round, heaving woman—
sun's rod for its divining.

Some rites have not
             mere metaphoric passage,
but are themselves the engine
spurred on by blow of buggy whip.
Some dreams surface
             in a certain summer
and ride the decades out without becoming
pale or less than their first glimmer.

Some dreams are more than dreams
             and taller than short stories.

She smiled across at me and asked
directions or instructions or . . .
this part is hazy, not remembered well . . .
Would you like to come with me?

                 She turned
on that heart-stopping exit line.
The door stayed open for eternity
then finally folded back in line.

I sat there. Stayed there. Twelve.

Still Life with Baroque Worries

SUMMER 1986

Pine tree roots
still crack the driveway
leaving long veined gutters
scrub clover has no trouble finding.

A cardinal collects old lily blooms,
runner twine from pumpkin vine
                    to line new nest.
The Downstairs Cat caught a sparrow
                        yesterday,
the rest is history.

Everyone's expecting the fallout
                from Chernobyl.
A neighbor hoards ice cream.
I lay in an extra bag of kibble.

New stars coming
will be waved ahead.
Poplars rake the Southern sky.
                    A squirrel
lectures from a fencepost pulpit.
The bright pink ribs of old azaleas
compete with honeysuckle condominium
                    for hummingbird's attention.
Yesterday the word went out
from maple to maple, dogwood to grass,
summer will be long this year
                    and unrelenting.
Everyone's expecting tax relief
                    followed by inflation.
A neighbor paved his patio
I have started counting chickens.

interval: The distance
between objects.

2

Shadow Players

Movers

We are always on the move
from natural world
to social tradition.
From little wars
to bigger wars.
Negotiated peace,
then off again to war.
The heart seems bent
            on traveling,
it thinks it knows
that any climate but the one
we choose to leave
has healing powers.

Some of us are leaving
              for California
when our ship comes in
or if the market holds.
Others simply take
possessions and themselves
to other rooms,
with different corners
than the ones before.
Four more dead ends
to bump up against
on nights as endless
              as the end.

Not to worry.
        Not to fret.
Mistakes are made
        in private now.
No one watches people,
only The Great Electric Window
              —and in stereo.

We are always going places.
Washington if we live
                    in Chattanooga,
St. Louis if we grew up
                    in Omaha.
Cherry Valley or the Hamptons
if we are quartered in New York.
Connecticut to get away,
Vermont to stay away.
Oregon to see what's going on.
To work. To school. To play.
To the market for replenishing.
To the wall to hear
what's going on behind the wall.
To hell if we're not careful.

Toward eternity, saint-like.
Toward oblivion, without thinking.
Toward fast-forward button
not daring once to push replay.
On and on toward the edge
to meet the other lemmings
                    at the plunge
look back if you dare
only Lot's wife's granite stare
returns your glances.

Mr. Peel's Way

Sorrow sticks
to his heel and toe
it will not come unstuck
even when he strides
                    through puddles.
He never thinks of it
                    as everlasting,
figures he stepped in something
                              once
that has to wear away with time.

He leaves a room
and if it happens to be sad
the room goes with him,
                        tags along,
follows like a fellow carrier,
wanting to catch up
figuring the two have things
                    in common.

Sadness
sauntering from street or sky
goes straight for Mr. Peel
as if he had some magnet pull.
                              He does.
He doesn't know it,
figures things are not too good
                              just now
but nests of swallows
                    bluejay babies
wait to be seen by him
if only all the trees
would pump life to their branches.
He knows they will. If not today,
                              tomorrow.
He has no affinity with swallows,
mother bluejay, bluejay kids—
only knows he's heard enough about
silver linings, bird song, rainbows . . .
they must make a difference.

He is only trapped
by what he's heard
saves convention's deepest bow
                    for Emulation.

He has been afflicted this way
                    always,
but thinks he can remember when
life was easy, smooth.
His shoulders didn't ache.
Always he is filled with logic
but cannot step outside himself
                    to see himself.
He is sure love is beautiful
because he has never been in love
and has no reference.
His life and how he lives it
                    were always obsolete.

No friends.
And so no obligations.
He is positive he owes everyone
and will get around to paying off
                                    the debt.
He has never stopped to wonder
why no bill collectors
                    press or haunt him.

He smiles through hardships,
does not believe in fate
but at the newsstand
thumbs, devours, memorizes
Popular Mechanics, Barrons,
astrology magazines—
keeps mental track
of Miss Jeane Dixon's
psychic premonitions,
pocket law, "how to's" on everything.

Mr. Peel's head
is a round compendium
of wot'sit and what-have-you.

He knows
that being sentimental
         trips you up.
He will not be tripped
or caught in snares,
is careful not to step over or across
things small or circular
not wanting to be catapulted,
left to hang
    in upside down position
        from indifferent tree limb.

On nights when he can sleep
        he doesn't dream
or know he's been asleep.
He keeps the radio,
the television, the lights on
        always.
Knows it is a waste
     of wattage
but figures he has them
     and ought to use them.

He is the advertising mogul's dream,
believing nothing's made to last
past Wednesday of next week.
Doesn't mind it. Accepts it
                              as *the way.*
Built-in obsolescence forms
                    the cornerstone
                         of his politic.

He believes in God
because he knows everybody does
                    and it's expected.
On the kitchen windowsill
chicken wishbones left to dry
pile up and threaten
                    sink below.
They will still be there
tomorrow and long after
because he trusts no one
to pull the other end
        of wishbone crotch,
and, anyway, he has not settled
                    on one single wish,
let alone co-wisher.

A bunch of trouble
was brewing on a sidewalk once,
saw him and fastened to him.
The dark around him
                    rails like harpies.
He knows the ringing in his ears
was carried forward from the womb.
                    He assigns no blame.
He believes that women
are quite lovely in the abstract,
refuses to pal around with other men.
He is not "in demand"
but he is not entirely invisible,
people notice when he passes,
he has an aura.
It would be the smell of death
if he knew how death smelled.
He doesn't. But it won't be long now.

Rimbaud's Sister

Rimbaud's sister still keeps guard
over the evil plants and garden,
letting the rain
do most of the watering
letting the sun
do all the hard work.
Here is the dark geranium
and there is the twisted mum.
Past the tongueless lilac bush
chalk lilies try in vain to bloom.
Violets sans scent or sentiment
strangle jonquils,
snuff out creepers,
eat at the ivy's underbelly.
Here where dandelion's Lord,
briar now resembles bluebells,
is only passive in the noon.

It isn't the earth
that you feel quaking,
merely the roots of nearby trees
sucking up stems through the dirt.

Rimbaud's sister arrives by taxi
always late in the afternoon
to give the honeysuckle comeuppance
and laugh at the cactus' open wound.
She's as mad as the crabgrass now
pulling the rhubarb out by its guts,
thrusting her hoe
in the hearts of daisies,
teasing anemones out of their stalks.

Passing the gate
you can watch the hedge
strike at the willow bending over
inexcusable in its race
to strip branch bare
before its time.
And that mad cackling?
                    Rimbaud's sister
urging the crabgrass not to be passive.
Take over the clover
once and for always.

Rimbaud picked a guardian angel
perfect for his purpose.
Who else could tromp
                    the zinnias so well
or sprinkle salt on the crocus?

She ministers to the aster's arthritis
giving it whiskey by the glass
and never a bird escapes the poison
she scatters to stop the daylily spread.

Those gnarled limbs
               set out in a row
were part of an orchard once
before she scraped their bark
                   to the bone,
kissed their buds with her foul lips
and kicked their shins till the sap ran out.
Cultivate thorns and not the rose.
Starve the plant so the weed can grow.

She dries pussy willow buds
soaks them in sugar and arsenic
a feed for the vermin
gnawing the hearts
of sunflower corpses.
Hear her giggle as the rats fall over,
staggering like a domino set up
in Japanese competition.

Rimbaud's sister
            keeps his garden
the way it ought to be kept
while he sleeps on through the ages
reputation intact.

To the Memory of Stan Kamen

Anton Webern died today.
On the gramophone he fell
in the second measure of a tune
not composed by him or heard
by the multitude who gathered
at the bedside of some lesser man.

Amy Lowell's been split in half—
first the lightning, then the rain.
Public domain might have killed her
but it never came to that.
Lay a wreath outside the garden
made of wheat and not of chaff.

Unknown soldier falling forward
onto ground still hard, uncracked,
bullets have no names upon them,
their mark is found by accident.
In the nest, the mother stretches
but still feeds every open mouth.

Georges Brassens' guitar is missing,
don't set out to find the thief.
Every day some music's stolen,
every hour some muse departs.
What's the use of wondering whether
art is simple; even art?

Anaïs Nin has ceased to scribble
life and times in common book;
turn your eyes toward horizons
you might have seen but haven't yet.
The morning post is late again,
the letter edged in black, unsent.

Ansel Adams' shutter's silent
as quiet as the hills he climbed.
Time's the winner in all races
even those against the times.
Another log on one more fire
so the torch will stay alight.

Franz Schubert has stopped pacing
schoolyards where his music wafted
from the student bands at practice
on the symphonies he made.
Only March, and here's the first rose
budding up from frozen ground.

Cheerio Meredith's gone away,
no forwarding address or note.
The actress melts into the scene
and gives the background body parts.
Friends still drop in unexpected,
add an onion to the stew.

The end of every day leaves something
if only promise of another.
Even gates now rusted shut
keep yards behind them safe.
Imagine what might not have been
if those we love had never been.

Passing Over

Finally clear of the treacherous air
he meets archangel face to face
demanding the peace he did not find
                    in life,
something hinted at
as life was moving from him.
He knows serenity is not
                the only state of grace
and yet it is the only place
where shadows do not haunt
                but compliment.
No more darkness, incandescence
            his only wish.
Put me to use by letting me sleep.
Give my speech to someone else.
Someone down there needing help.

Cloud be my protectress
now that the wind has stripped me bare.
I need only a little air.

Greeting those who went before him
he hands out leis of beatitudes,
is mindful of old enemies
                          coming on as friends.
So this is the way it happens—
all things rectified, all ends tied up.
If only he had known the truth
deep in his darkest nights—
that life was only a passing over
                                into life
instead of a silent prayer on airplanes,
the awful crawl toward religion,
life not life except in fleeting.

Los Hombres

FOR CESAR VALLEJO (1892–1938)

They come before dawn
with rifles and dogs
and fenced-in flatbed trucks,
a man has to be
a fool to be caught
unless he's asleep
or making love
(both forbidden
  if one would live).

Bandits they are
with beards over ears
smiling as each ripe head
    they crack open
spills its watermelon seeds
and rolls down to the gutter.

Early this morning
they killed a guitar
and laughed as its splinters
                    split the air.
There is no armor
against Los Hombres—
their bayonets slice steel.

And where are
the carpenters of the sun
when the mob comes riding in—
lost or dead or locked away?
Poisoned in beds
without turning over
to meet their destroyers' eyes.
And all the funeral gardenias
                    are dead
used up in an earlier revolution.

Lion Watch

Here in the night
we knew would come
our voices have all gone silent.
No songs now
and worse—no singers.

Here is my hand
take it and come
down to some other country
as spears of silence
cut up our shadows.

Hear the wind blow,
it's shaking the cradles
it's rocking the stars,
knocks at the moon.
Nelson Mandela come home.

Pierrot Lunaire

Two ducks park on the common,
        a pair of shiny boots.
Nearby a woman who has spent
the morning feeding swans
shakes the final crumbs
            from paper bag.
No more, my darlings. No more.
A moorhen runs across the water.

Just down the street
old crumbling cottages
stand amid staked hollyhocks.
Old plants, these,
with pale young flowers
deep enough for single bee
to spend the day in unobserved.
A bricked-in sapling
that long ago grew into tree
shades cowslips rioting
amid the millweed and the clover.

Monsieur Lunaire looks up.

What's another tone or two
up or down, more or less,
before you tackle,
wrestle to the ground all twelve.
One won't matter to the grass.
Human voice as instrument
does not produce remark of praise
                              or banishment
from drifting clouds;
              the clouds move on.

The head can only take in so much.
                    About a headful.
It then regurgitates and takes it all
                    back in again.
This tickling of the intellect
produces no great laugh.
But oh, the smiles an unplanned
just-right note solicits
and gets back.

From the alley comes
a family with a picnic basket.
Another Sunday in the park with Arnold.

I know not whether Pierrot
will meet his Pierrette
or if the long-neck rope will be
the final lover who goes thoughtless
                        to his lover's bed.

Using *moonbeams as a rudder*
or *wine that only eyes can drink*
is gross misuse of moonlight.
Love dies. So what about it?
Music goes on living.
                Chopin side by side with Cage.
It's not the fault of Freud or Dr. No
that one ear listens better than the other.

The stereonucleosis is the cause
                        of the effect.
Eat your sandwich, Arnold.
This is ham, Arnold. This is cheese.
Put them together, you've got
                        hamoncheese.

Variety Artist

Always balancing,
highwire walking.
Clown yellow over
                    Kabuki white.
Taps on soles,
souls on tap.
Bring fish and chips
in Variety wrap.

Oneliners fall
or fly like confetti,
or drift like down
from an ostrich fan.
The followspot catches
the hare in the hat
that turns into harlequin
doing handstand.

Always scrambling,
ticket in hand,
spangles sewn over
holes in tights.
Dreams on hold,
hold on to the dream.
No jealousy twixt
the man and wife team.
Easter week
at the Oakland Orpheum,
pulling it off
that's variety art.

Still Life with Rubber Washer

Don't know when
I'll be back,
        she said;
don't forget to tape
        "The Colbys"
and any thirties movies
you think I haven't seen.
Cats need their shots
        in two weeks.
It's only a splinter
in Drago's paw,
just coffee stains on the rug,
soap and water will lift them,
merely a crank
who calls the second line
        and disconnects.
Kitchen faucet only needs
        a washer,
don't call the plumber,
pick one up at Koontz'.

Ticket for the cleaning
is under the sugar bowl
            in the kitchen.
I know you won't worry
            about me
but don't anyway—
(this part of the note
was an afterthought).

And I thought
after reading it
that she forgot to say,
Have a nice day,
write if you get work,
hang by your thumbs,
take off five pounds,
don't take any wooden
Susan B. Anthony dollars.

Sure,
everybody thinks about
            dying.
It's only another progression
each of us is moving to.

She forgot to remind me
about changing the baking soda
            in the ice box,
watering the ficus,
turning the porch light on
            an hour earlier.
Vote, she said.
don't bleach printed T-shirts,
write your congressman,

                    pray.
Only lately have I thought about
            dying alone.
Won't mind it much,
I don't think,
not much choice.

Could have done things
differently or better.
Could have prepared,
taken out different insurance,
put a few bucks in the bank,
treated the kids
                a little better;
listened to them more.

I could have
gotten over you,
before you got over me,
          or could I.
Sure,
And it's not too late
to rethink life.
Maybe after I've pulled
          the thorn
from Drago's paw,
and picked up the cleaning.

interval: The relation of tones
with regard to musical pitch.

3

Is There Life After Tower Records?

Is There Life After Tower Records?

FOR RUSS SOLOMON

It had gotten
          on to five o'clock.
She dropstitched traffic
                    down the Strip,
where everywhere a different tuner
tuned to a different FM band
rose and mixed
              and clanged against
a different Southern California
                          wall.
Top-down weather made
the sounds more howl than cry.
And each is paramount
as Paramount once was.

In front of her
              she saw his face
his eyes inside his lookback mirror.
As descriptions go, he was ordinary.
As ordinary as the stars
spilling dust from other worlds
then coming back
for second stardust strafe and drop.
He was as plain as gossamer must be
          to secondary angels.

He smiled, she thought,
or anyway looked back
and caught her staring
                past his shoulders
trying hard to see
straight through him to forever.
And at once the traffic
and the hour was unimportant.
Nothing. In perspective.

The car in front of her
                moved forward
and she was pulling up
beside the man astride
the gleaming two-wheel steed.
Closer. One long sideways,
heart-stop, close-up.

Is this what Continental thunder
                means,
arriving at the right place
                and on time
if only once in what we call
                forever?

And now she knew
what God looked like
and why His image
had never been explained.

God threaded traffic
to the next stoplight
and as He did,
the silver spokes of His machine
threw rainbows in the sunset
half down Sunset
bounced off fenders
                to wide windscreen,
ricocheting from back bumper
                up to front
polished hubcaps,
dry-humped radiator decoration.
A thousand stars spread out
and caused as many halos,
birthed another thousand,
                thousand stars
that split into long lines
                of dots and dashes,
S.O.S.s, distress signals,
                warm caresses.
Incredible illuminations.

Where Sunset turns
              and forks
                      divides—
right for pop, left for classics,
God made wide turn
into pop parking lot
as suddenly as Deities
turn tricks to converts.
She watched resigned
              as if confirming
that all her life was being spent
                      in limbo
                          the wrong,
and never made right lane.

God was into pop.
              She was into classics.

TWO

They grind perfectly.
In balance always.
Move in closer,
listen—hear the cylinders
clicking inside
well-oiled inner cylinders.
Sleek and slick,
perfect wheels in perfect motion,
their precision every bit as good
                    or better
than the not-so-public
                    public works
in fire hazard factories
on the edge
of hidden business districts.

These friendly robots
in designer jeans
and ties too narrow
to be tied just right
have heard mind-mending music.

Each has seen
the Tower beacon light
that draws them forward
like the final candle
on the last, long earthbound
                        night
before the sudden
exclamation point
preceding blindness.

Not to follow
        this young piper
in the red and yellow suit
who beams the true light,
                pipes the noise
is to miss not just the
                        newest
Mozart Angel Compact Disc
but something social
                that once gone
does not come back
the same way twice.

Some women
and some younger girls
track time sans telephone
                and clock,
they chart the hours
by how many business cards
each collects, exchanges
on nightly Tower Records
                            trips.

Some men come from
                    Bakersfield
some drive all night
from Salt Lake City,
Phoenix, Reno, Abilene,
to browse, meditate,
worship at the L.A. shrine.

They say the queue
at Tower 1 in New York City
goes half around the block.
What discotheque or synagogue
could boast such popularity,
such an ever-constant, faithful
                            flock?

See them move
between the aisles,
pathways so narrow
that passing past another
is bold adventure,
thrilling drawing-in
of breath and stomach.
And in between the aisles,
the islands back to back
that hide the million dreams
                              inside
bright jackets,
          well-turned sleeves
plastic fused so fast
it must be cut apart
to reach the shiny metal hopes,
the deep dark vinyl of delight
whose inner grooves can only be
decoded by the diamond needle,
narrow beam of laser light.

Piano, piano, dolce Carlotta,
do not break the silence, Tom
as Hildegard of Bingen's song
pipes softly overhead.
Listen easy as the alto sax
skips down between
the bars of Gershwin's
        Second Rhapsody
                to freedom.

It could be
there will one day be
Towers on the edge
of every continent.
Great meccas where
the lost, the lonesome souls
caught in between the coasts,
in what each nation
proudly terms its heartland,
can come and trade
those bushelsful of unmade music
locked away restrictions,
and unlocked-at-last anxiety.

For now,
the coasts of North America
are the only ports
equipped with Towers.
All across the land
in summertime or chilly winter
you can see bold stickers
on late-model foreign cars,
old Ford trucks,
and Iacocca's pride and joys,
I left my heart in San Francisco's
                              Tower,

I gave my heart away
in the L.A. Tower parking lot.
I ♥ New York's Tower.

THREE

A crowd was pressing hard
                against, around
                        the new releases.
The Telarc bin was under siege.
Long thin men in suede stood guard
while their molls talked
                        playing times,
argued over merit versus price
and in hushed whispers
spoke of leap by Shaw/Atlanta
across the aisle to Pro-Arte.
Ah, block vote poor Berlioz—
        is this thy sting?

She passed an older couple
                fussing with
the new/old Furtwänglers,
moved down the aisle of Polygram
                in time to hear
a woman's verbal cruise of clerk:

I am not sure what name
                                    it goes by
but it's from a symphony,
I think, an opus, something.
I can hum it for you, if you like.
Did you see the movie "Frances"?
It was playing on the radio
in her apartment when she took the pills.
Speaking of radios
                    you have a strong chin.
Anyway, it was an opus something.

She went directly to Rachmaninoff
(not daring to address
his dour countenance, Serge).
There she stood, bent over,
                        Botticelli-like
fingering Ashkenazy, caressing Bolet
                        and Gavrilov,
pausing to feel Richter,
lingering over Horowitz,
Wondering if Cécile Ousset
would ever be released
on Compact Disc.

Had Kocsis completed the concertos
                and the Rhapsody?
Were they still in the Philips vaults
or still inside his head
                awaiting word
on vacationing de Waart?

Did Ashkenazy live walled up
inside a glass recording booth?
All that Rachmaninoff
                and Sibelius,
and Brahms, and Mozart,
                        Prokofiev too.
The Chopin, Mussorgsky—
what a busy man he was.
She liked his hair. Its texture
in the black and white photograph
reminded her of the green stuff
that passed for grass
in old remembered Easter baskets.
More than once she thought about
                a trip to Iceland
(his new home country)
                as an act of homage.
She even knew the cost
of round trip airfare.

Martha Argerich looking out
from all those jackets,
lovely and demented.
Did she choose Nelson Freire
for Rach's four-hand piano suite
because he played so well
                                or because
he looked like such a hunk?
Every month she rifled
the newest *Schwann,*
The Green Catalogue,
                    imported *Gramophones*
hoping to find a solo CD
by the blond mustachioed Pelias.
Nothing. Nothing new.
Martha kept him locked away.
She pictured this young male
                                Rapunzel
waving from some turret bedroom
to every passing hunter/huntress
hoping for a rescue
from mad Martha's eighty-eights.
She knew that come some quarter,
Harry would reveal it all in print,
wasn't that the reason why his fury
                        and his Sound
were both termed Absolute?

Her reverie was interrupted
by a sampling of *Glassworks*
from the speakers overhead.
Anxiety sprang up
from shadows still unformed.
It smothered her, erased all thought
                         of muscled Frenchman
in a single brittle clanging sweep.
Another twenty measures
of what sounded like a rivet gun—
her head was throbbing,
                         pounding with it.
Clearly she could see
the whole Glass *oeuvre.*
Hundreds of music sheets,
thousands of repeat bars,
millions of collective headaches.

Coming round the corner from Serge
past Strauss, Strauss family,
Tchaikovsky, Telemann, Torino
she neared Vivaldi and
the many-but-none-different versions
                         of *Four Seasons.*

She thought about the total manpower
needed to make Canadian Brass,
the Pipers of the Royal Guard,
the Soviet Army Choir,
the Kronos Quartet.

Rubbing by
a man of no certain age,
but wonderful,
absorbed in miscellaneous Ws,
she felt the numbing start—
round her ears at first
then dropping down
            to ease her neck
then down below
and down below that
and down.

Suppose she died this minute.
                Imagine.
This was heaven,
she'd be in it.
What if she only fainted?
Opening her eyes he'd be there.

She moved around the island
till she faced him.
Her heart slid from her body,
            rose up above the racks
and hung there in the air
                        between them.
(Hearts and other body parts
do that sort of thing at Tower.
I, myself, have never seen it
but more than one eyewitness
has told of Tower para-normal.)

Here was not the nomination
                        the candidate,
the darkhorse running,
                        not even winner,
but The Award, as platinum
as all the records rumored
to be framed and hung
in Quincy's L.A. mansion.

By open non-apologizing stare,
she surveyed all of him at once,
became the rodman holding pole,
                awaiting signals.
Eye through telescope.
The telescope itself.

Soft as grassblade underfoot,
strong as stars at nightwork overhead,
gentle as the one thing missing
that plagues our eyes
                and haunts our ears.

Jessye Norman
was now wandering through
The Four Last Songs of Strauss.
Yes, I am ready for the nighttime
anxious for the day ahead.
Come and meet me
in the sky's round ribcage.
Come and melt with me
through eyelids closing
on the red clay dust of life.

The hair that curled up
from V-line of his open shirt
matched the color of his bushy head.

Both hands cradled
the album notes he read
the way a father holds
                    his firstborn.
He brought out glasses
and she saw his hands, big,
a half-caste brown.
Because his head stayed down,
                    bent over,
his eyes, whatever color,
continued as a mystery.

Jessye Norman purred
Beim Schlafengehen.
Yes, I am ready to receive
                    the starry night
I will give my sensibilities
                    to sleep.
Um im Zauberkreis
der Nacht . . . Tief und
tausendfach zu leben.

There you are.
Getting near the Telarcs
          was hopeless,
but Stereo Review, D.A.,
even Ovation and Fanfare
loved Muti and the Phillies.
Auger sings on that one too.
Is she becoming a Carminalite
                    or what?

Anyway, I got it.
The man of no certain age
          and the woman
                    turned
went through the turnstiles
into *die gestirnte Nacht.*

How weary we are of wandering—
Is das etwa der Tod?

—ON BEHALF OF THE MANAGEMENT—

Tower wants your business
and wants to be your friend.
Come here where the Angels practice,
away from budget-minded Seraphim.
Where the Denons speak in tongues
the Orfeos descend
and many RCAs are sixty minutes-plus.

Here is where the stopped heart
                    is revived,
the heart that races, slows.
Where more than records spin
and at many speeds.
We exist to fill your needs.

No exchanges without receipts.

FOUR

Because *need* is stronger
than the pop star's fans
        the diva's claque,
those who come before these spires
to spread and spend their need
will keep returning, coming back.

Plastic is not transitory
it does not decompose.
So all those red and yellow bags
crying out from subways, sidewalks—
I have been there, I am going back—
will go on rallying the flock
long after St. Martin's
is no longer in the fields.
Some may worship
at a brand new Wherehouse,
a few espousing licorice
                    over aromatic tea
will go where seekers of
        the Licorice Pizza go
as they went off
                in search of Peaches
and the Record Bar.

As always, out in California
new prophets will appear,
some will follow Aron,
others stay with Solomon.
A few will send long lists,
                love letters
to that Casanova of the disc,
                André Perrault,
quels sont les nouveaux discs?

Nipper and the Brothers Warner
                may sleep uninterrupted
through Carlo Tessarini's upcoming tri,
this year's Webern triple-header,
but Chandos will stay wide awake.
Phonogram has started making boxes
        for unlimited boxed sets.
From Hilversum to Hollywood,
the rally cry goes up . . .
A box in every house.
A house without a box is not a home.

See how the Francophallic Angels
are tugging at Maurice,
come put the toot suite André touch
on Carlo's solo trumpet piece—
wise André's holding out
for the comfort of Continuo.
A harpsichord, cellos maybe,
                    a violin or two
(makes counting easier,
              covers up the wobbles).
It's that or else
a host of Angel Voices
and Nancy Allen's harp
through oval walls.

Gottfried Heinrich Stölzel
will find his share of trumpeters.
Marsalis will collect
his yearly Grammy (yawn)
to the cheers of millions
who love their jazz classique.

Each disc in its own jewel box.
                    Tamper-proof.
Supply must ever march
ahead of mere demand.
New releases will be pressed
                    as cut-outs.
Hurry. Get your copy of the Double Concerto,
Lenny and Herbie the dueling maestros
have put Deutsche back into
                    Grammophon.
Alas, the last black vinyl *Schwann*
                    sailed off
before the cover shot was ready—
no down or underfeathers rest
          beside decaying analog.
The digital distance deepens.

Who built the Tower? *We did.*
And who is that new release
behind the small mustache?

FIVE

At intermission time
on the Opera Quiz last Sunday
William Livingstone was asked
what role, if any,
he would like to play
and in which opera.
He mentioned a small
                but significant part
where the hero gets killed early,
                dies gloriously,
and is talked about incessantly
all through the next two acts.
The hero always dies
or never is, she thought.
She looked around the room
for heroes. There were none.

Maybe she had picked
the wrong time to arrive.
Late night was only good on weekends,
and only for looking and appreciating.
Of course, appreciation was a part
                of "the experience"—
but afternoons or early mornings
were friendlier. More easy.

Never any sense of competition
                    in the mornings.
The music too was better.
Beethoven in the background,
                    Vaughan Williams.
(The lark always ascending.)
Bach partitas, two-part inventions,
Papa Haydn at just-right volume.
Scriabin sometimes. Sibelius.
Nothing too experimental.

It had taken months to learn
certain rules about the game.
The close-out section
was reserved for students,
those on budgets
who confined themselves to budget lines.
Greensleeves. Eminence.
            Privilege. Odyssey.
Greensleeves fit them.
            Odyssey did not.
Eminence and Privilege
described their lack of either.

The older, mind-set crowd
        browsed opera bins.
But opera buffs were square
        or over the top.
There was no in-between.
Some of the most interesting, alas
liked only Callas, Berganza.
Sutherland, Schwarzkopf.
Horne. Sills. Dame Kiri.
No room for mortal women
                in their lives.

The well-dressed ones,
        approaching thirty,
only cared about
the basic repertoire,
crash programs in the classics.
Go home with one and be prepared
for competition with Vivaldi.
Fantastique translates to
the Gallows March,
playing it the only element
                of danger.

Musicians and the money group
gather twice a week
to check each other's bins and buns.
They carry Mahler scores
                    in leather cases,
whistle Bartók, hum the counterpoint
to each Slavonic Dance,
own every version of Brahms *1st*
assigned to record since fifty-five,
can prove to you Ravel fucked up
Mussorgsky's *Pictures*
by adding all those band parts.
They have never heard Smokey Robinson,
the Maddox Brothers and Rose,
                    and never will.
Roy Acuff will remain a mystery
long past *Times* obituary.
Some ignore, dismiss Rachmaninoff,
with whom she had a secret kinship—
strengthened by a Tarot reader
who, looking at her cards
                    and fingers,
informed her she was the Russian
                    incarnate.
AND, he died in forty-three
the same day she was born.
Some things are only buttressed
                    by coincidence.

In the Tower
it was best to move around.
Invent the storyline yourself
for the burly one in alligator boots
who carried off an armload of CDs
devoted only to castrati arias
transcribed down for trombone solo.
Imagine why the little man
                          whose hand shook
bought four separate versions
of Bach's *Cello Suites,*
two *Brandenburgs,* and seven
                          (count them, seven)
picture postcards of a young Ned Rorem.
And who is the lady on roller skates
and why is she looking at me?

She looked up from a reverie
induced by Göran Söllscher
                          playing *Cavatina*
the door was opening.

Always something different's
                    noticed first.
One time it's eyes, hands, or thumbs,
then speculation as to size
                    and what size means;
nothing, everything.
Sometimes a bulge around
                    the middle of a frame.
This one was at the perfect distance
to showcase all of the above.
A minute later, less. He was not alone.

She stayed only a little while more.
Picked out the Parrott
                    Monteverdi *Vespers,*
a Gruberova French recital,
paid for them by credit card,
watched as they were
eased into the so-familiar yellow bag,
left without a turning back
and started driving home.

She had both Sills samplers now,
the Callas *Norma* and the *Carmen*,
the Chopin set from last week . . .
still, there was so much music
                    at the Tower
new releases all the time.
And as she drove she thought about
        tomorrow's Tower hour.

A click. The trapdoor opened.
And then the blazing laser light.

Still Life with Horne and Sills

Some butterflies
will not be choked
by chloroform or cyanide.
They soar beyond the corpsman's net,
the mason jar that lies in wait
to stop them from their jet stream ride.
Why bother living if life means
        that means to end is specimen?

He thought of Hairstreaks under glass
as he sat on a summer evening
        listening to Kodály's
        Summer Evening.
The day had been as gold as gold days get,
sun oozing butterscotch across the garden,
squirrels teaching alphabets to birds
        too drunk on one another
            to be listening.
Morning glories adjusting
        to daylight savings time
and he as tender of a flora/fauna flock
that strayed to roadside
           and the neighbor's yard.

The *Summer Evening* music nodding
                to a close
he tried to choose between Madame Sills
and Madame Horne as "doing dishes"
                         atmosphere.
She of the soaring Verdi
or she of the rising up then dipping down
                    Rossini.
A compromise. Bubbles for the washing
and the rinsing off, Jackie for the drying
               and the stacking.

Some butterflies, he thought,
              are cunning,
knowing nylon net as well as silken
               spider webbing.
They tread nature's traps
and never end as threading.
A butterfly saying under its breath
give me a task and I will find
       a way to divert its completion
was his kind of moth, not likely caught,
skewered by White Coat Warden or Black Widow.

For too long now
the awful sense of throwing time away
had colored every day and night
                    he moved through.
And while he wasted time
he knew that Time was wasting him,
                    enjoying the process.

He got up, went to work, came home,
                    cooked, gardened,
                        exercised always,
went to bed, got up, went to work . . .
Did all the etceteras he had done
                    for always.
In the mirror he saw no one different,
though daily he looked in looking glasses
            expecting someone different
                    to look back.
A Substantial Other, maybe,
though friends were that one luxury
that had always been beyond his means.

Madame Horne was dropping down the octave.
He dropped down on fours and gave Nobody
                        twenty.

Men's muscles move better
when their souls are making
                    merry music,
having La Horne on one's side
produced a lighter sweat from push-ups.
He got up light-headed, almost dizzy,
replaced Rossini on the record player
                    with Stephen Foster,
allowing Marilyn to dream of Jeanie,
                            beautifully,
expound on hairs vs. fuzz
and take him to the Camptown Races.

The summer was in every way
                    the way it should have been.
Fat bass cruised the surface of the lake,
minnows in their wake. Geese came back.
The bee balm bloomed, dead-headed,
                    budded, bloomed again.
Nasturtiums entertained the hummingbirds.
Beverly Sills presented *The Pearl Fishers,*
He traveled to The City twice to see it.
And every night for him alone,
she and Mr. Victor Herbert told about
        the sweet mystery of you know what?

Music was his discipline
far into June and then beyond.
He bought loudspeakers for the garden,
snap shot day lilies at their morning peak
while Sills/Horne lured and lullabyed
　　　　　　　　the birds and passing traffic.

He knew each butterfly that flew the yard
　　　　　　　　had only so much time
and yet their numbers seemed to grow.
Like lilies, those with deeper hues
always came out deeper in the season.
August brought the lovely ones, the stars.
Art is calling me, I want to be a Prima Donna . . .
Like Madame Sills and Madame Horne, in song,
　　　　　　　　they were so in silence.

Some words, like love and death and hope
　　　　　　　　and immortality and music
are overused by all of us. He stumbled,
　　　　　　　　　　　only once.
'tis the gift to be simple, 'tis the gift
　　　　　　　　to be free . . .
Horne? Sills? They had long ceased being
　　　　　　　　　　separate.

interval: A space of time
between any two points.

4

The Lower Forty

Pacing Off the Lower Forty

And I said to him, *call me.*
Not too early, not too late,
call before you come
with gifts of interruption
and impossible requests
for friendship, cups of sugar
green tomatoes, cans of Flit.
I'm on deadline. One of many.
You want sympathy? I haven't any.
                      And no time.

If there were time, real time
I'd figure out a way to say IT
(that thing still lurking
in my head someplace
should be said or shouldn't)
without resorting to book writing,
the agony that has no ecstasy
                    at other end.
With time I could invent
                experience anew
and not go on depending
on endless reinvention.

Just now
all favors have been called
every borrowed minute has been used.
And still last contract book stumbles
on familiar ground without an ally.
Could the poet
        even die on deadline,
meet God's schedule
        better than his own?

Stuff still moves into my rooms
        willfully and without bidding.
It crowds me out, demanding time
away from work that has no pleasure.
Here, then, some answers
        to waiting correspondents:

If you are out of red, send the blue.
Enclosed my access number and regards.

The answer to your question is, I would
but not with so many unwashed watching.

Remove my name from Franklin Mint
mailing list. Thank you.

I love you too, but in another way.
I'll die if I'm not held again or do holding.

Please send catalogue of 50,000
classical lps described in your Fanfare ad.

Dear Michael: *Uptime* is the only speed
my doctor approves of. Send case.

Excuse me from performing jury duty.
Shoot the bastards.

Visiting Japan again in October.
Please arrange meeting with head of Sony.

Purple Rose of Cairo, Yellow Rose of Texas,
Rosemary's Baby. Don't know other seven.

Whitman because he liberated the language.
Sandburg for keeping the language intact.

I like Jiffy peanut butter because
I want to win the million dollars.

There is almost always
something better to be done
than writing books or letters.
The garden sends an invite.
At three o'clock the Four o'Clocks
make ready to reopen. Be there.
And at the garden's other end
violence has moved from street
                    to melon patch.
New headlines fly in from the meadow:

DICHONDRA INVADES BABY TEAR
IN BOLD GROUND COVER FIGHT

* * * * *

SLUGS CAUGHT AT SITE OF
HALF DEAD HOSTAS

* * * * *

APHID GANG ASSASSINATES MR. LINCOLN

* * * * *

FERNS FRY IN HEAT ATTACK

And so I go off through the grass
to cheer on Johnny-jump-ups,
Polaroid snapdragons
and slice spice branches for a stew.
Tomato vines in need of feeding
wilt down in mock suicide
until I mix narcotic fix
(2 parts Spoon-it, 1 part Miracle-Gro).
Cucumbers are all leaves and vine
                from too much water
their fruit mere pimple-pricks.
No one's trimmed the backyard hedge
so Century City's disappeared again.
                      Hooray.
Enough new rhubarb now
           for rhubarb pie.
Two gardenias open
      on a bud-filled bush
and I've not filled a single page
          with sentence scratching.

I leave the morning glory
                    and the ivy
to mid-morning mayhem,
pack the cats off with head-scratch
                    and belly-rub,
heat the coffee, close the door,
Rachmaninoff at the ready
                    I begin again.

      The bull of Minos
      stumbled blind
      and fell on fours.
      Kind Ariadne . . . shit . . .

I could let it ring. I will.
No good news is on the way—
the lottery is two months off.
One day, pretending circumcision,
I'll slice the telephone's umbilical
                    straight through,
till then, God damn Alexander Graham.

A stack of unread papers
and others set aside
            for second reading
has grown another foot.
Recipes and regimens
under rosary paperweight
rearrange the dust in living sculpture.
I say my prayers. I brush my teeth.
I think of all those things
            I should be writing down.
All this is exercise enough
to tire poet, prophet, annotator.
And there's a salad to be tossed,
a four-line rhyme to set aside
                        or hide.
The potted thyme has mealybugs
the potted sage has withered
the potted seed has gone to pot
and I am not who you imagined.
I imagine I am someone else.

It is the telephone again
insisting I am here when I am not,
such conceit to ring out interruption
as if it were worthwhile endeavor.
I will not surrender to unthinking bell,
                                not ever.
Give in once and it's all over.

        Kind Ariadne's apron opened
        scattered shells in dust
        bull-man heard the bells
        and charged the coast.
        What maze—

A new song spews
from dreaded Westlake School for Girls,
it shatters through the hills of Beverly
blotting birdsong, loon chorale,
Mozart sonata practiced in the music room,
                low bee-buzz in lily.

Not cherubim or seraphim
but Sean's Madonna in a workout
              on school pornograph.
Pile driver beat kills couplets.
Overdubbed shah-na's smother sickly muse
so tired of all these rewrites
she now calls in trumped-up excuse
                          for absence.

The cats are back from cupboard sleep,
hunger's hit two hours early.
Pollen waits till now for sneak attack.
Where's the tablets? Where's the justice?
Where's the highway through the maze and out?
Ariadne's somewhere spinning
closed to any thought of help.

Radio

FOR CHARLES OSGOOD

The archers aim,
the straining bow,
the whistling arrow
through the air.
The victims cry,
the awful fall
as body and earth
meet up as one.

The trumpet bridge
that moves us then
to stratagem's hall
behind the line.
An argument, then
a new war plan.
Our Hero's foot
on the marble floor.

And now a harp
as lovers meet
a last embrace
a close of the door.

Here in your head
you saw it all
without the blink
of camera's eye.
You were the victim.
You were the winner.
The falling soldier,
the arrow spinner.

Yours was the mind
conceiving the plan
to win the battle
by hour's end.
You played the harp
and the voluntary,
colored the sky
and the hero's hair.

Amazing the sights,
springing from sound
that move unbound
through the air.

Outside Tres Vidas

A MEMORY, JANUARY 1975.
FOR GERALDINE ROBINSON

These holy maidens,
polygamic brides
of God's only son,
hurry through the square
their Father-in-law
        has summer-blessed.
All starched linen hats
and dark-hued habits,
they stride like rondo
    in Mozart sonata,
from worship to worship.

Inside the oval hole
cut out of their dark
morning, mourning clothes
to give their faces
exposure and a chance for air,
they mumble prayers
while in the act of walking.
So goes the praying
to and from the act of praying.

A donkey being led
in opposite direction
bows low as they pass by.
All here have Latin mania.
Even animals are Roman Catholic.

Somewhere a serenade
and lovers waking
to a new prognosis.
Love is not a dire
and scandalous emotion
but innocence gone off
beyond corruption,
back to innocence again.

Lovers do not waste
their precious time
looking up original sin
in ancient history books,
they loll on hillsides,
embrace in squares,
and make a morning coffee
                last till noon.

Vendors on their way
               to market
carry sausage platters
               on their heads,
balancing babies on their backs
and string bags filled
at the ends of too-short arms.
These women with congenital
                    lopsided heads
made so by carrying world-weight
down through the centuries
have not changed their gait
                         or posture
since Pope I started
               earthly reign.
Even those not widowed
               still wear black.
It is as close
to Christ's bride's habit
they can come without the vow
                         and ring.

The men
are hard at work
in their first siesta.
They will rise at noon,
drink warm, early wine
then settle back again
in slumber's arms,
protected by remoteness
and somnambulism.
No demons dance
inside the heads
of lazy-boned and fat
young guardians
of town square
whose doze is done
to keep tradition
moving slowly,
without complication.

Melons ripen
needing not
the watchman's clock
         and gaze.

Our daily bread
has been provided
        by provider.
The job prospect
is best left to those
for whom prospecting
is vocation. The fool
who somehow managed
to do battle with
and conquer his siesta.

By the sea hotel
where crab rolls out
of conch to stroll
uninterrupted to the shoreline,
a seagull, not hungry,
but a glutton first—
seabird later—
snaps the many-legged creature up.
A fine *hors d'oeuvre.*

Back at the conch shell,
| VACANCY |
is hanging out again.

Faith as fact and with
no trace of mystery
is practiced here
by everything that crawls,
slouches, walks erect
or with its head bent over.
Even morning tide
says the *beads*
by bringing in
            and taking out.

This village is eternal
squatting on the map between
            Heaven and the Abyss,
not in purgatory surely
but well this side
of Heaven's Gate.

On these rosary days
repetition,
not locked doors,
is the sure security.

Old wooden angels guard
the newly carved
and brightly painted
pine trunk Christ
whose arms stretch out
to meet the nails
without a flinch or spasm.
The church around this brand-new
                    folksy artifact
is not completed yet. But
first things first. Christ's head
is not so bowed he cannot watch
the bricks on either side of him
being made and set in place.

Some evening when
the angels both have nodded off,
Christ will turn his head
toward the ceiling
seeking further orders.

When death arrives
in this hilly hidden place,
it is not depreciation
but mere calculus.
But no one speaks of death
and the only non-believer,
truth,
is most unwelcome guest.

Have You Been to Holland?

Have you been to Holland
to Friesland where the locks lie open
and North Sea meets Atlantic?
Following Rembrandt on the night watch
as gulls give windmills helping hand
to Rotterdam, then Amsterdam
through acres of petals
                    firm and proud.

Have you seen the tall ships
waiting for tide and wind in measure?
Fishermen fondling nets like lovers,
brothers all of the mother sea.
Sisters all of guarded land.
Children each of the Heavenly Father,
protector of this marched-on place
every neighboring country covets.

Who grows the bulbs, sails the ships,
builds the dikes and in between
staves off armadas from Aragon?
Only the Dutchman tall and proud
guarding the land through centuries.
Here in this beautiful stopping place
invaders wisely call Netherlands.

First You Take a Live Goat

Maybe those old emperors
with mechanical canaries
                    had it right.
Turn on the music
only when you have to.
Don't make a habit
of summoning muse,
call her only out of love
or desperation. Or both.

Life
seems to be a little like
authority—always too much
or too little. Overbearing,
and never there when needed.
Always laughable
but never funny enough
            to laugh at.

Modern Romance

Every/one
is taking
temporary
measures.
Paper plates.
Carbon paper.
Water colors.
Cupcakes
instead of
cakes.
Crumbs
instead of
loaves.
Naps
to keep
from
sleeping.
Tranquilizers
in lieu
of poison.

Cardboard.
Mortarboard.
Bored.

Every/where
gestures
supersede
movement.
Batteries.
Feather
dusters.
Filters.
Pegs
on doors
instead of
padlocks.
Bandages
instead of
treatment.
Television
to keep
from
talking.
Psalms
in lieu of
penicillin.

Synthesized.
Traumatized.
One size
fits all.

Every day
a little
closer to
the edge,
a little
farther
from
the center.
Solo.
So low.
Lonesome.
Loan some.
Meantime.
Mean time.
Indivisible.
Barely
visible.
Invisible.

And
the Angels
sing.
Listen!
You can
hear
them.

Everyone
is taking
temporary
measures.
Everywhere
gestures
supersede
movement.
Every day
a little
closer to

Still Life After All These Years

FOR JERI SOUTHERN

How is it now
at a quarter past three—
difficult, lovely, painful, good.
The moon on the lake is especially nice
                in middle age or otherwise.
All of the intervals meeting at once,
                those in music,
those in time, those that cross
and meld in the mind. *Coming together,*
staying apart, lost in diversions
                dancing starts.

Friends remembered, new friends made,
old friends dependable whatever the hour.
Not every dream fulfilled.
                But not every dream thought up.
Always some new door opening
the same day an old one closes.
Mama buried for fourteen years
and still the bush throws off roses.

Still the romantic
                believing love
the brick, the mortar, building block.
Handel discovered, Mozart renewed.
Mahler and Bartók at last understood,
                and I lived to see it.
My own concertos moving along
(not fully aloft, but not moribound).
Part of the perimeter Rachmaninoff,
but room for Stravinsky,
                the Copland crowd,
the widow of Weill, the sons of Strauss,
Ella, et al., both Marsalis boys.
                Endless lists in a life unending.

And what of the fires that burn awhile
and then go out without mystery—
is there regret, a shrug of resign,
bafflement at lack of warning,
                a cry, UNFAIR?
All the above and more.
Bewilderment. Betrayal.
                Self-hate swarming.

But, there are the travels
through difficult books,
            unfriendly lands,
torment at the hands of experts
with a last minute fall into grace.
However thick the mind gets with thickets
there's always a clearing,
            a twang of birds,
a black leopard cat
on his way home from Zion
who'll give you a ride on his back.
Still one more Autumn to crawl through.
Still one more Alice-hole-in-the-wall
            to fall through.
And always and ever *au suivant*.
The next and the next, and the next
            after that.

Indelible impressions,
            like digital audio tape,
some of the soul is missing
but everything clear and in shape.

Sighs, not breezes. Songs unlike wind.
Nothing coming easy. Everything redefined.

If there's a creed
          floating over it all
(this nonsense and stuff
to be gotten through),
its some kind of love into everything.
Some kind of selflessness
                    out of self.
A kernel of truth distilled from the lie.

If someone rocks the cradle
be glad it's not the ark.
If someone falls and will not rise,
          still run to help him up.

Because I cannot fill every want
                    my needs are more.
My wants are greater each time out.
But I have nothing any more
               I would not exchange,
                         or give away,
for a little more talent,
          a little more time,
a little more sense of focus.
Focus is the juncture where it all began
                         to unravel.

Legend says that Li Po tried,
      while drinking in a boat one night,
to reach and grasp and hold
           the moon's reflection . . .
Alas, he lost his balance, fell overboard
          and drowned.

Any poet worth his words will tell you
the moon on the lake is especially nice
      in middle age or otherwise.

INDEX OF FIRST LINES

Always balancing, highwire walking 62
And I said to him, *call me* 111
Anton Webern died today 49
Autumn comes early 19
Don't know when 64
Every/one is taking temporary measures 133
Finally clear of the treacherous air 54
Have you been to Holland 130
Here in the night we knew would come 58
Here the eagle lost and weary 20
How is it now 137
I close the windows 3
In the interval between bed sitting chair 11
It had gotten on to five o'clock 71
Maybe those old emperors 132
Pine tree roots still crack the driveway 28
Rimbaud's sister still keeps guard 44
Some butterflies will not be choked 103
Sorrow sticks to his heel and toe 37
The archers aim 120
The old A train 24
These holy maidens 122
They come before dawn 56
Two ducks park on the common 59
We are always on the move 33
We drive back late from supper 16

Rod McKuen was born in Oakland, California, in 1933. At eleven, he left home to work at jobs that took him throughout the western United States as rodman on a surveying unit, cowhand, lumberjack, ditchdigger, railroad worker, and finally rodeo cowboy. His first attention as a poet came in the early fifties, when he read with Kerouac and Ginsberg at San Francisco's Jazz Cellar. After serving two years as an infantryman in Korea, he returned as a singer of folksongs at San Francisco's Purple Onion. Before becoming a best-selling author in the 1960s, McKuen had been a contract player at Universal Studios and a vocalist with Lionel Hampton's band and had amassed a considerable following as a recording artist and nightclub performer.

His books, numbering more than forty titles, have been translated into some thirty languages and make him the best-selling, most widely read poet of his time. His film music has twice been nominated for Academy Awards *(The Prime of Miss Jean Brodie* and *A Boy Named Charlie Brown).* His classical works—symphonies, concertos, suites, and song cycles—are performed by leading orchestras and artists throughout the world. *The City: A Suite for Narrator & Orchestra,* commissioned by the Louisville Orchestra, was nominated for the Pulitzer Prize in Music.

He has written songs for nearly every important performer in the music business, producing standards that include "Love's Been Good to Me," "Jean," "I Think of You,"

"The World I Used to Know," "Rock Gently," and "I'll Catch the Sun." A nearly seventeen-year collaboration with Jacques Brel that McKuen terms equal parts of translation, adaptation, and collaboration produced "Seasons in the Sun," "If You Go Away," "The Port of Amsterdam," "The Far West," "I'm Not Afraid," and two dozen other songs. Those compositions, among others, have earned the writer-composer-performer more than forty gold and platinum records worldwide.

Rod McKuen poetry is currently taught in schools, colleges, universities, and seminaries around the world. He is recipient of the Carl Sandburg and Walt Whitman Awards for outstanding achievement in poetry, and the Brandeis University Literary Trust Award for "continuing excellence and contributions to contemporary poetry."

In addition to his poetry, the author writes for United Features Syndicate and is a contributing editor and reviewer for various audio/video magazines including *Digital Audio, Video Review,* and *Stereo Review.* Throughout his life, McKuen has been a record and music collector, and is considered by many to have one of the world's largest private record collections.

He lives in Southern California with his brother Edward and three cats, Bingo, Magic and Niki. Asked about future plans, McKuen mutters something about winning the California lottery and giving up all this nonsense.